You did it!

Practice tracing and writing the number.

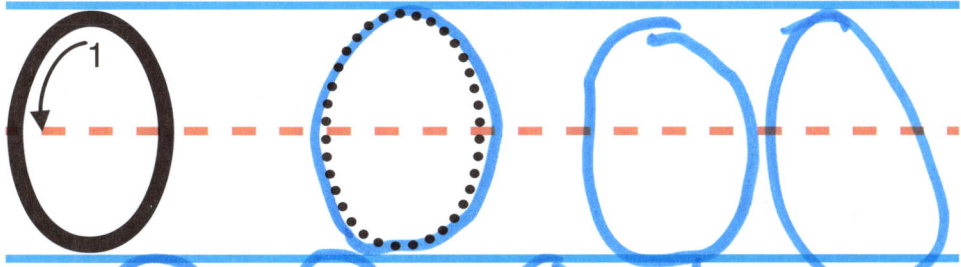

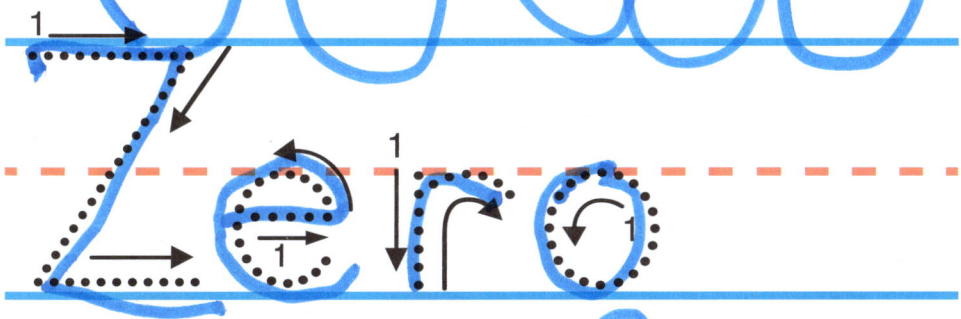

0

zero

In each row, circle the bowl with the least number of fish.

Practice tracing and writing the number.
How many alligators are there?

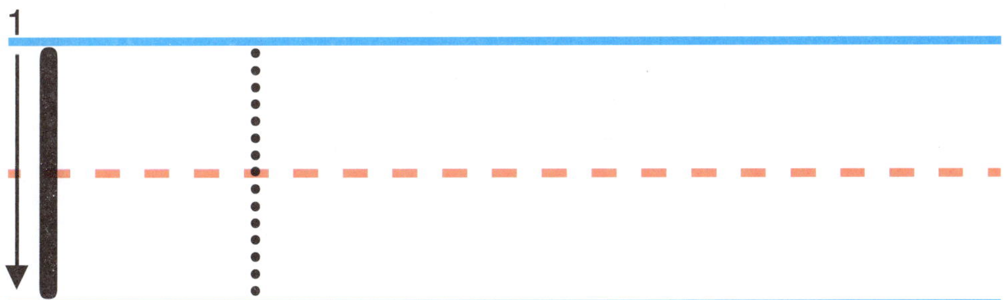

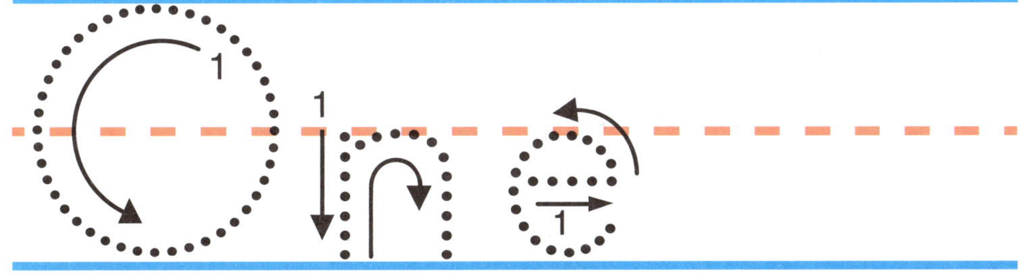

0 1 2 3 4 5 6 7 8 9 10

Practice tracing and writing the number.
How many elephants are there?

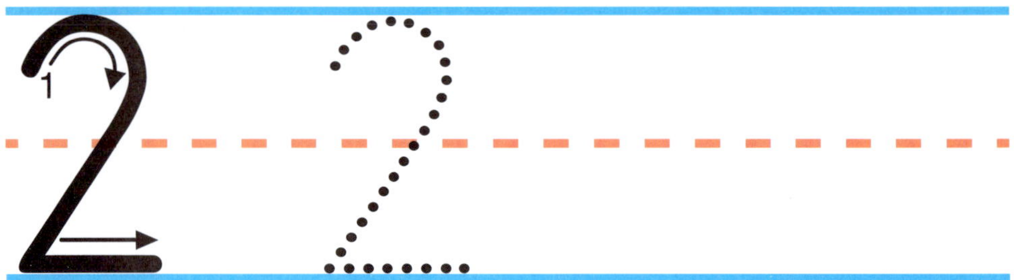

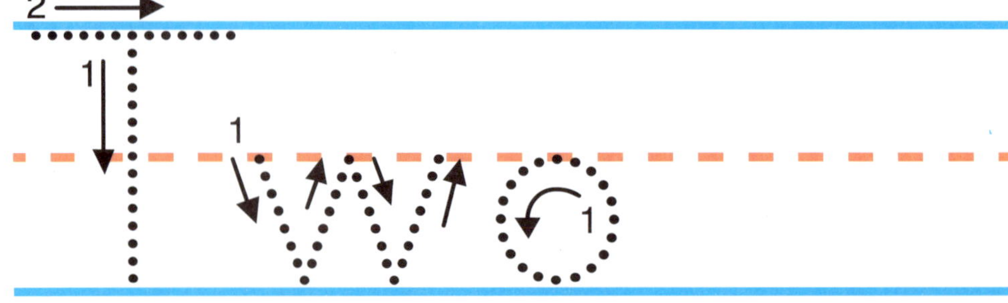

Draw a line from the number to the set with the same number of elephants.

1

4

2

3

You did it!

Draw lines to connect the sets with the same number of objects.

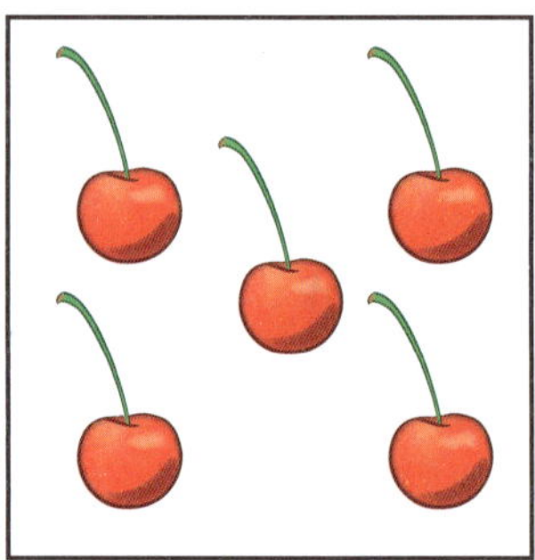

Practice tracing and writing the number.
Then color the chickens.

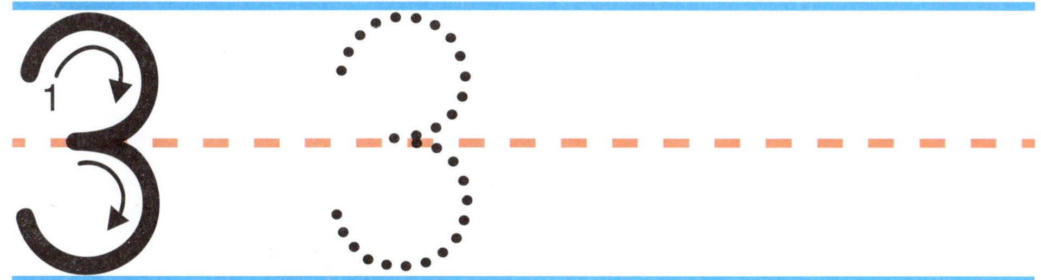

Three

0 1 2 3 4 5 6 7 8 9 10

Count the animals in each row.
Then write the number on the line.

Practice tracing and writing the number.
Then count the trophies.

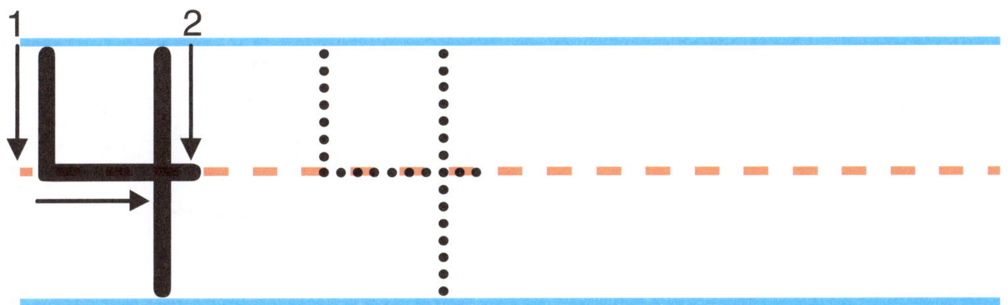

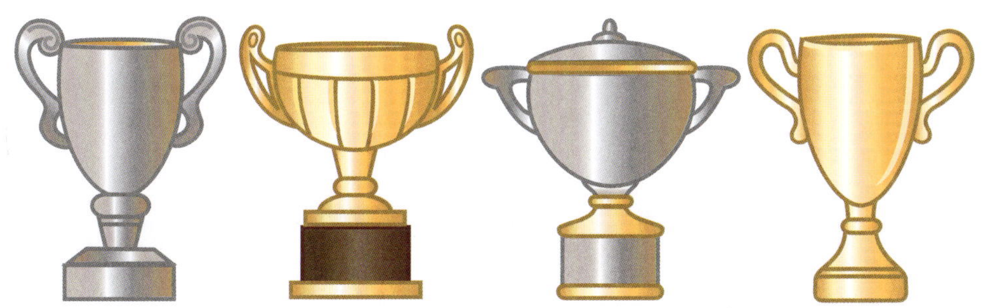

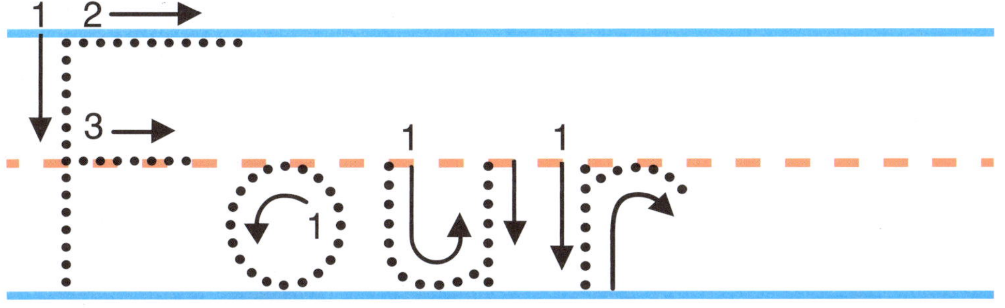

0 1 2 3 4 5 6 7 8 9 10
Draw a line from the number to the set with the same number of objects.
2
3
4
1
You did it!

Practice tracing and writing the number.
Then color the birds.

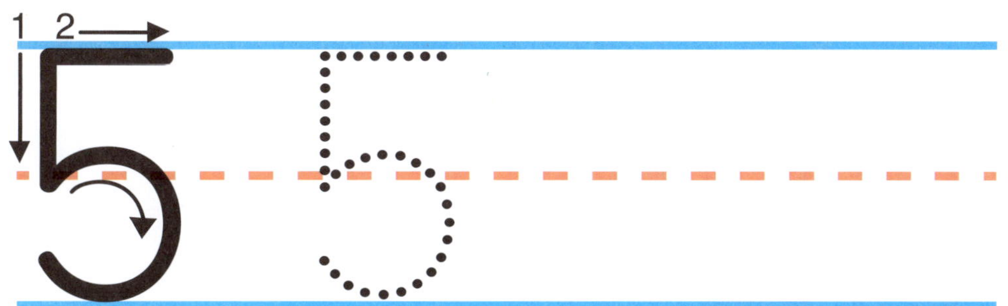

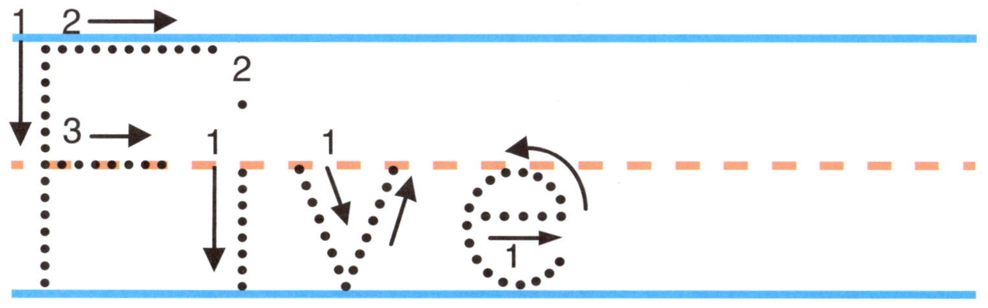

Count the shapes in each box.
Draw more shapes so that each box has 5.

Draw a line from the number to the set with the same number of objects.

0 1 2 3 4 5 6 7 8 9 10

Write the correct number for each set of objects.

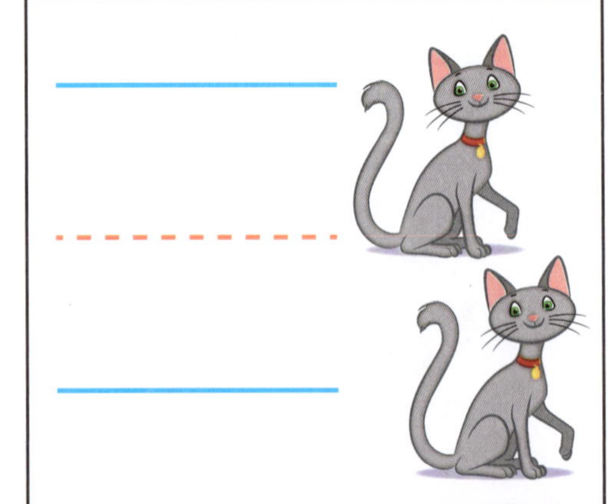

Look at the number in the box.
Circle the same number of objects in the row.

0 1 2 3 4 5 6 7 8 9 10

Practice tracing and writing the number.
Then count the guitars.

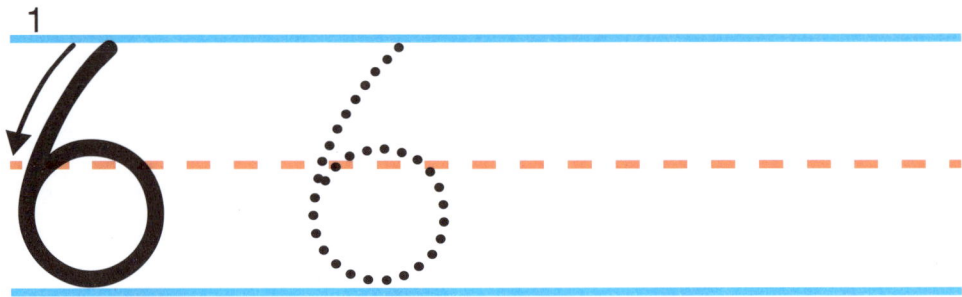

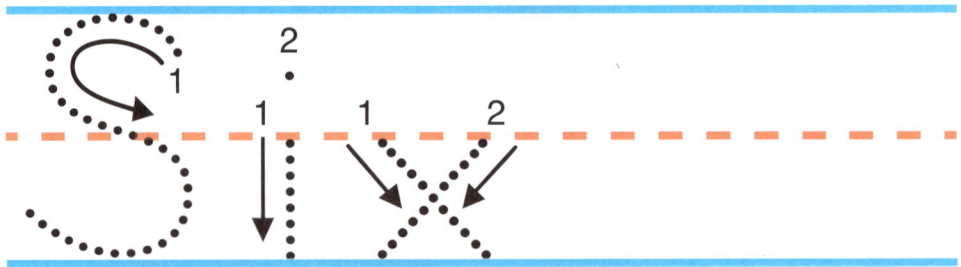

6 6

Six

You did it!

Write the number that is one more than the number shown in the first circle.

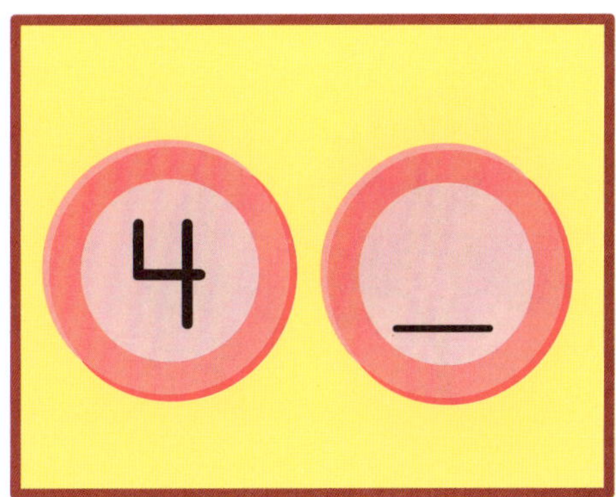

Count the number of trees in each row.
Then write the number on the line.

Count the number of flowers in the garden.
Then write the number on the line.

______

______

______

0 1 2 3 4 5 6 7 8 9 10

Color 6 animals in each row.

11 12 13 14 15 16 17 18 19 20

Draw a line from the number to the set with the same number of objects.

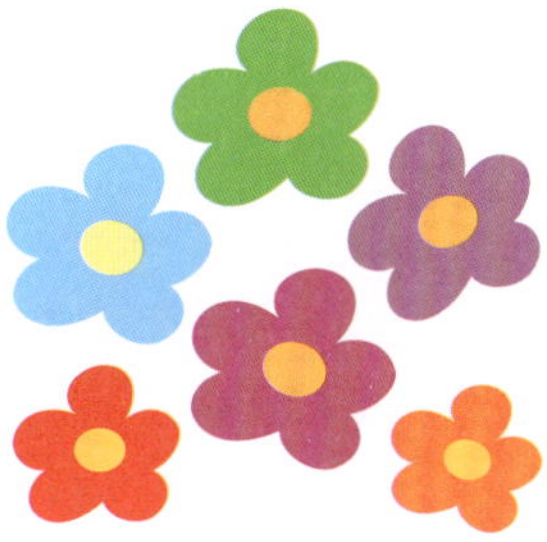

1

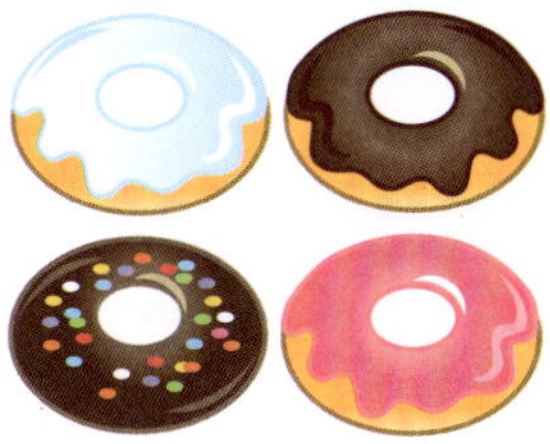

2

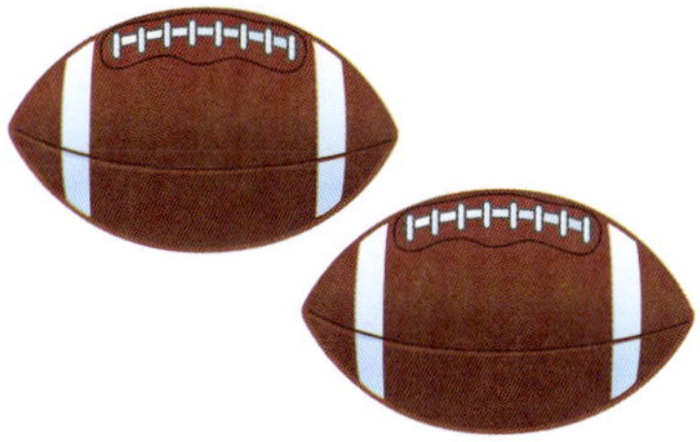

4

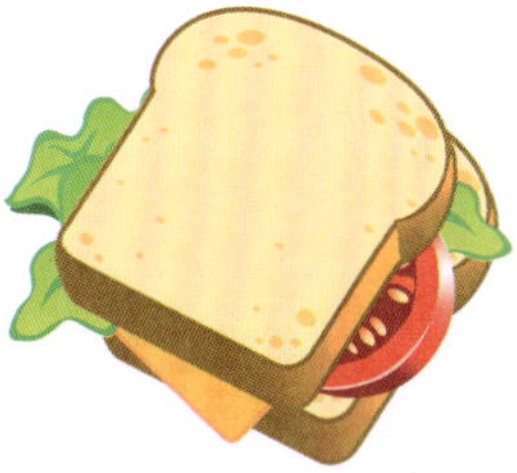

6

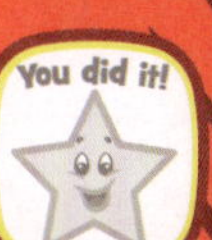

Practice tracing and writing the number.
Then count the cows.

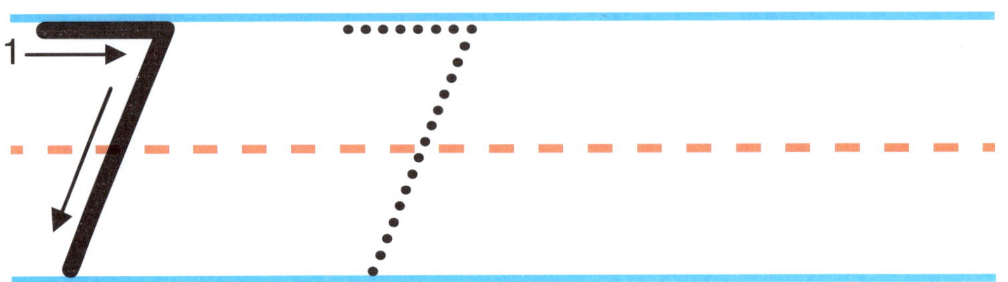

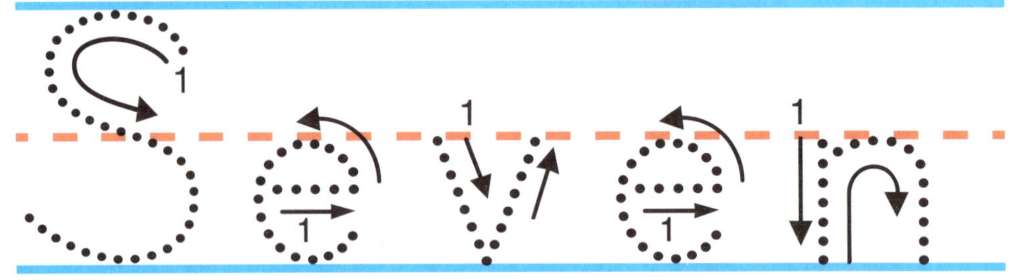

Circle the group that has less than (<) 5 objects.

0 1 2 3 4 5 6 7 8 9 10

Counting forward, write the missing numbers on the blank lines.

1, ___ , 3, 4

0, ___ , 2, 3

3, 4, ___ , 6

1, 2, 3, 4, ___

1, ___ , 3, ___ , 5

4, 5, 6, ___

2, ___ , 4, ___ , 6

4, ___ , 6, ___

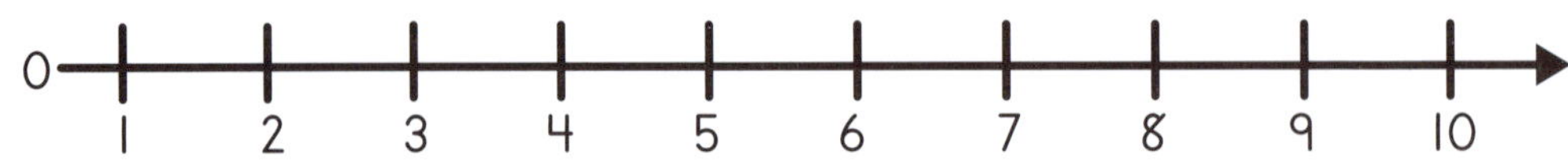

Practice tracing and writing the number.
Then count the kids on bikes.

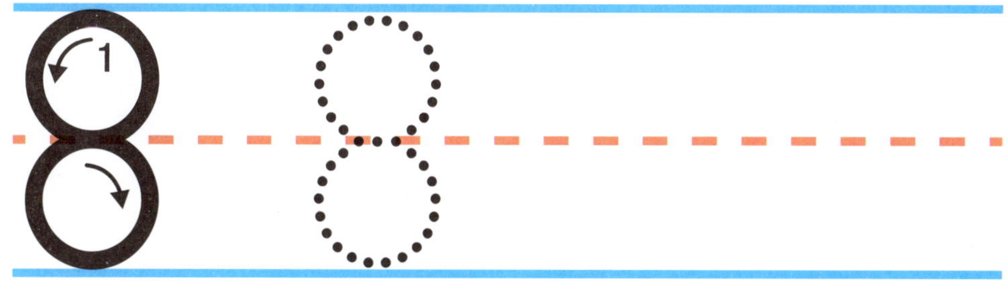

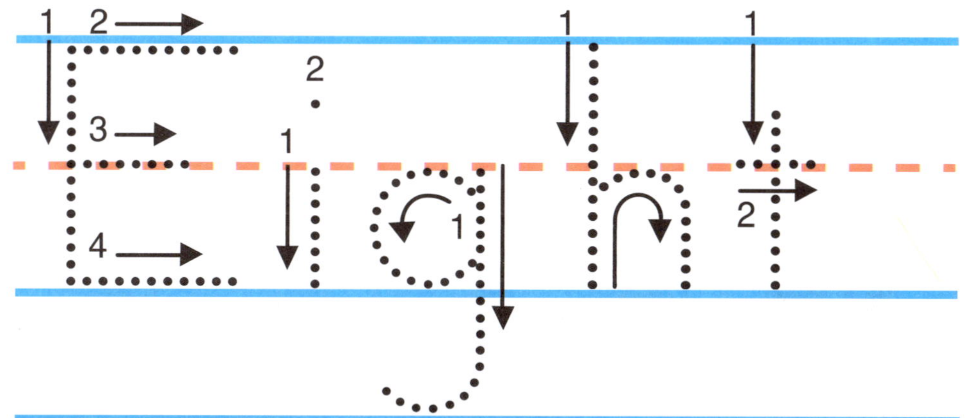

Draw a line from the number to the set with the same number of objects.

6

7

4

3

You did it!

Count the shapes in each box.
Draw more shapes so that each box has 8.

0 1 2 3 4 5 6 7 8 9 10

Connect the dots in order 1-8 to finish the picture.

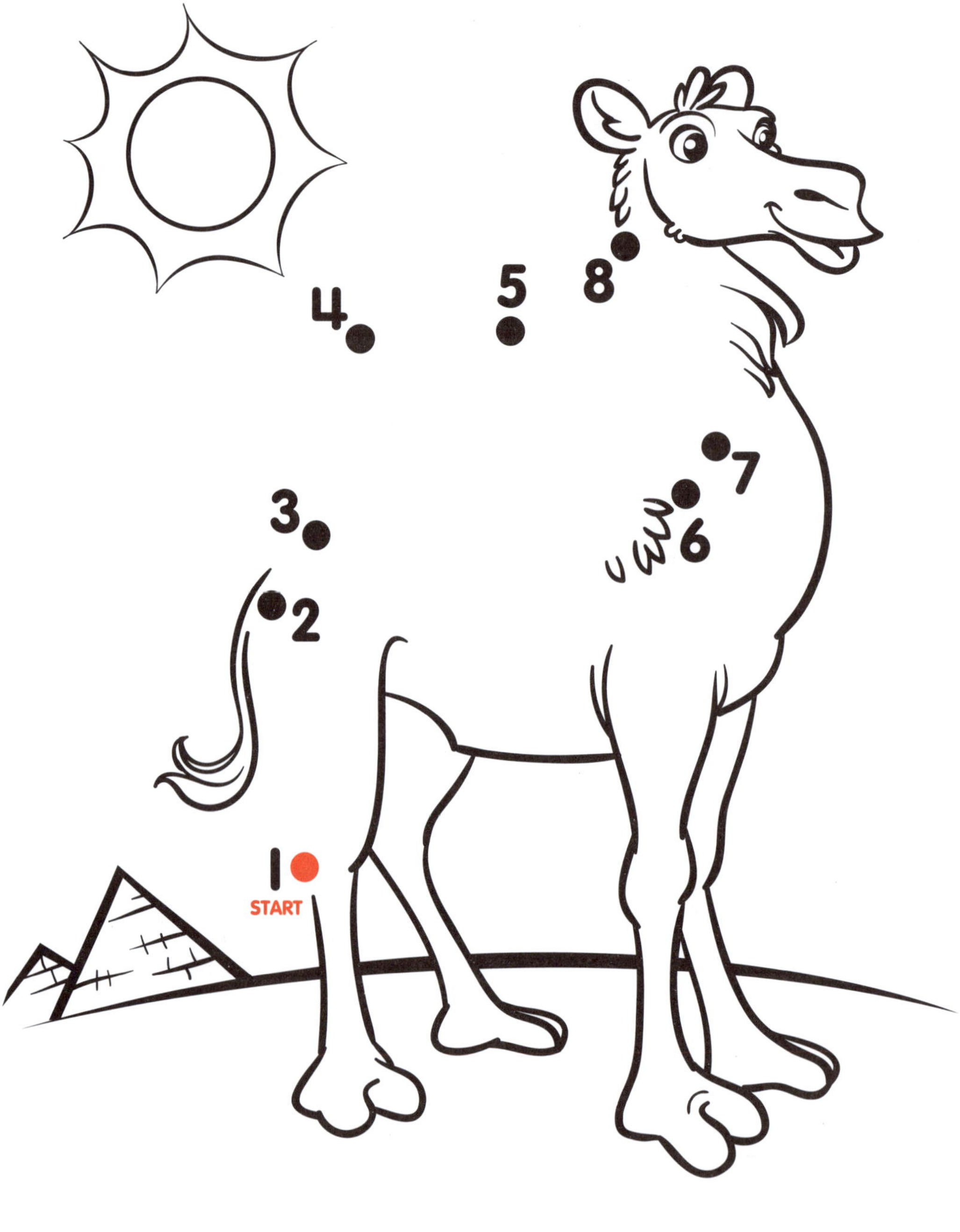

4 5 8

7

3

6

2

1

START

Count the number of ducks in each box.
Then write the number on the line.

______

______

______

Practice tracing and writing the number.
Then count the vehicles.

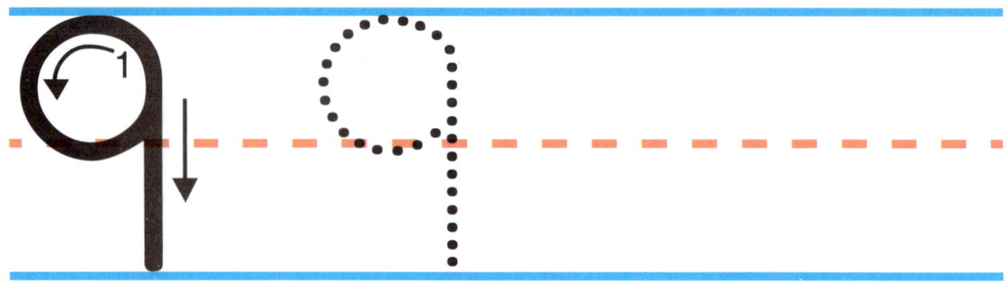

Nine

Count the number of objects in each box.
Then write the number on the line.

____

____

____

0 1 2 3 4 5 6 7 8 9 10

Counting forward, write the missing numbers on the blank lines.

5, ___, 7, ___

7, ___, 9, 10

___, ___, 7, 8

1, ___, 3, 4, 5

4, ___, 6, ___, 8

7, 8, ___, 10

0, ___, 2, ___, 4

4, 5, ___, 7

Practice tracing and writing the number.
Then count the butterflies.

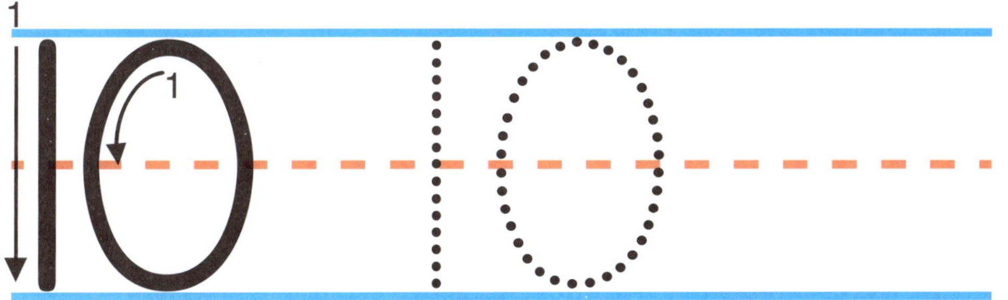

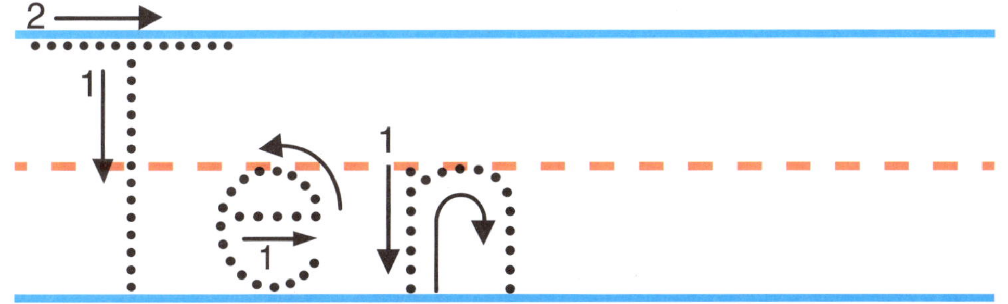

0 1 2 3 4 5 6 7 8 9 10

Color 10 of the balloons. Make 4 red, 2 blue, 2 purple, 1 pink and 1 yellow. How many of the balloons have no color?

Connect the dots in order 1-10 to finish the picture.

Color the picture by number.

1-Purple

2-Green

3-Yellow

4-Orange

5-Blue

6-Red

11 12 13 14 15 16 17 18 19 20

You did it!

Practice tracing and writing the number.
Then count the lollipops.

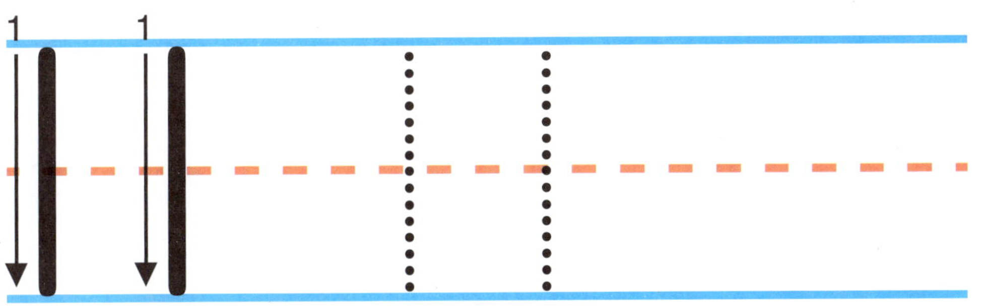

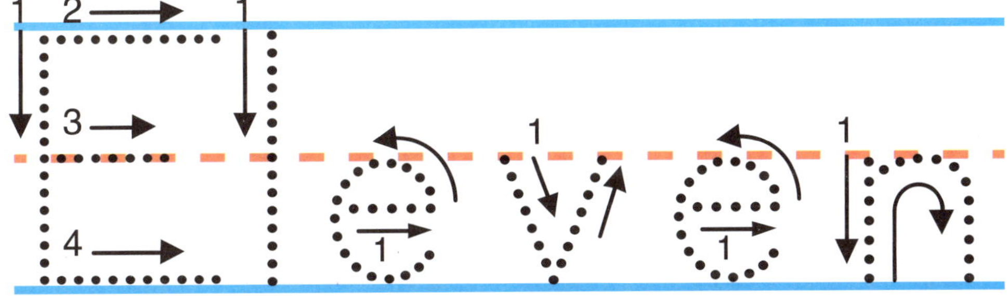

Help the cat find the path through the maze to the finish.

START

FINISH

Practice tracing and writing the number.
Then count the frogs.

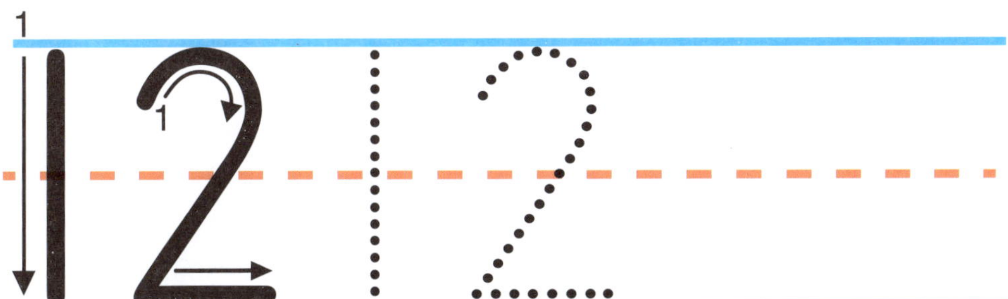

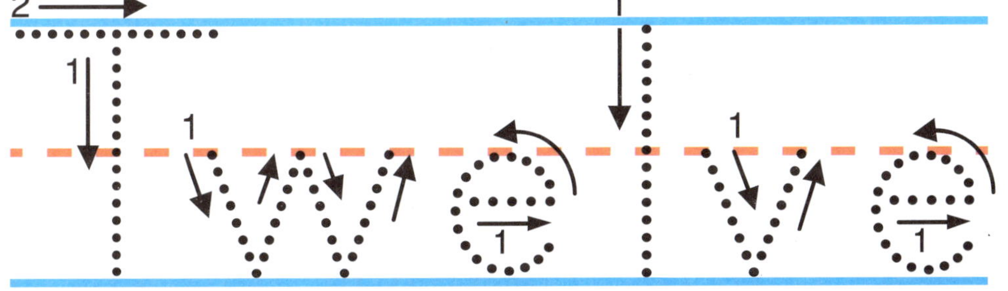

Color 12 of the puppies on the page. How many of the puppies are not colored? 12 + __ =14

Count the objects in each box. Then write the number on the line. Circle the groups with less than (<) 10 objects.

Practice tracing and writing the number.
Then count the deer.

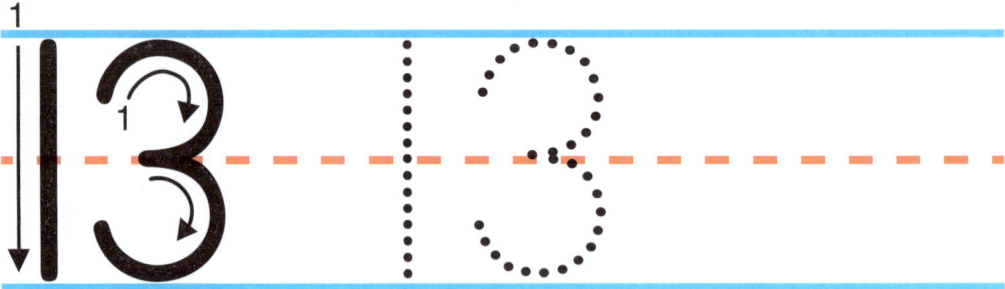

13 13

Thirteen

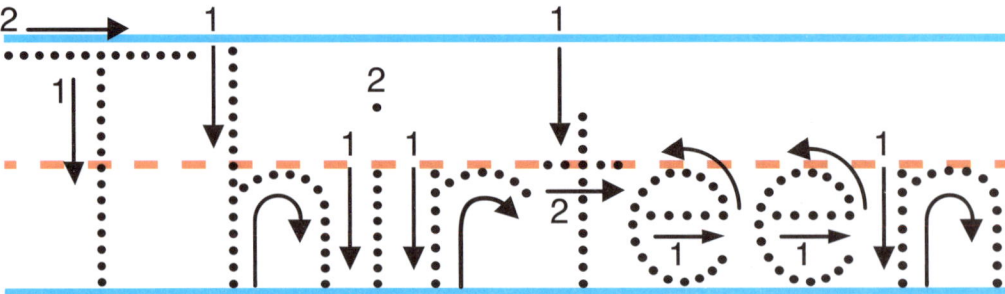

Here are 6 hats. Draw 7 more hats to make 13 hats all together.
Color in the hats.

Practice tracing and writing the number.
Then count the ladybugs.

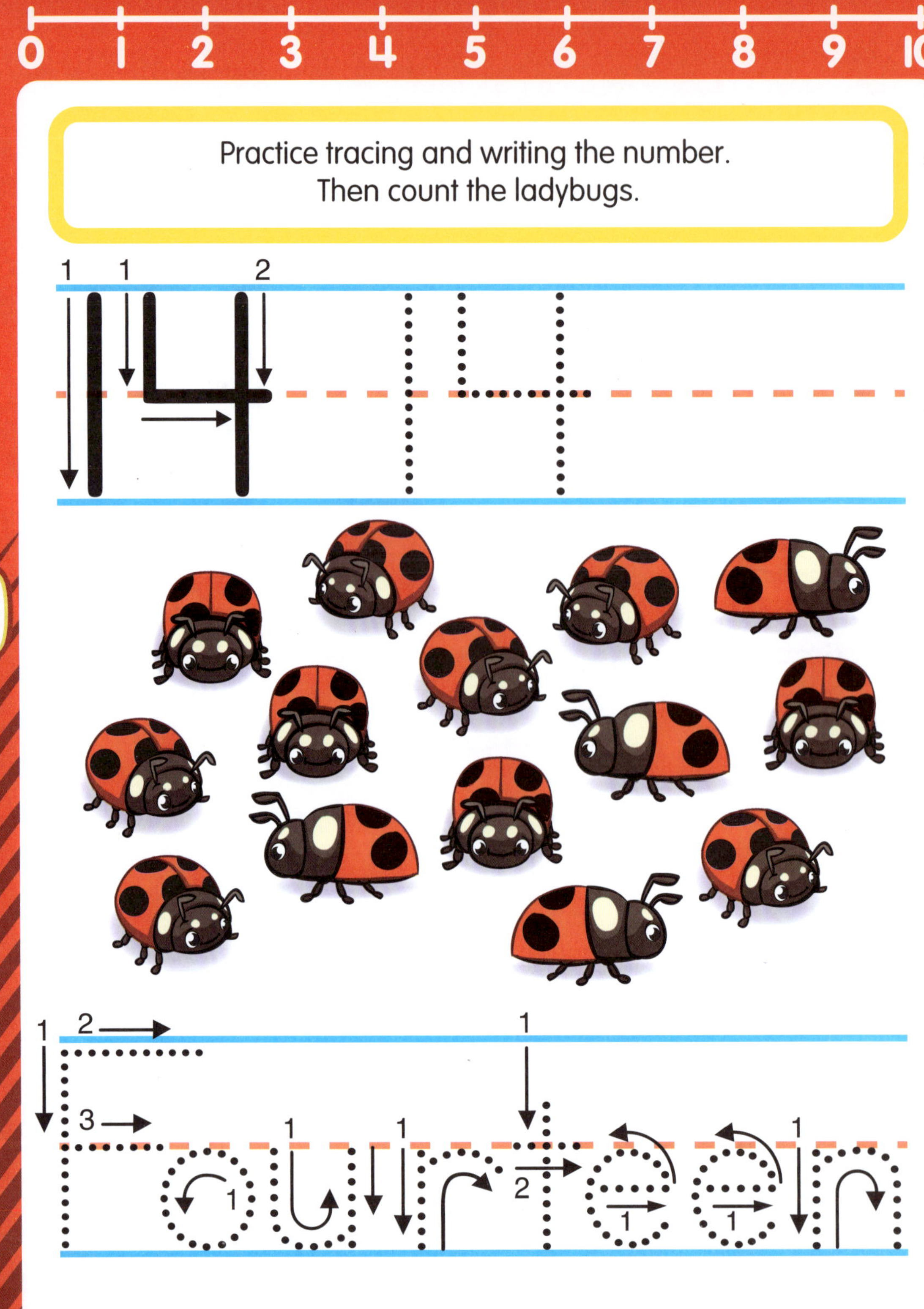

11 12 13 14 15 16 17 18 19 20

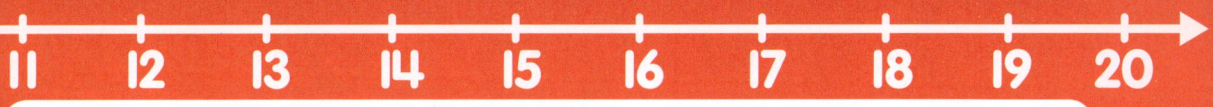

Draw a line from the number to the set with the same number of objects.

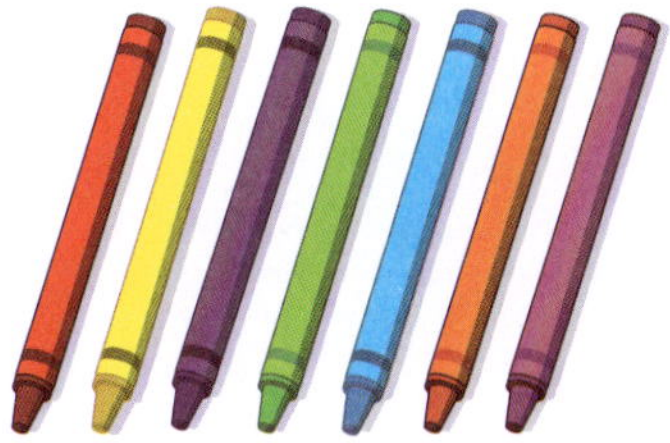

6

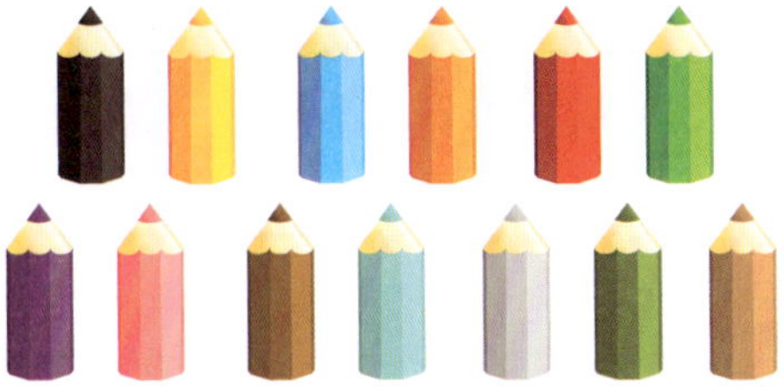

7

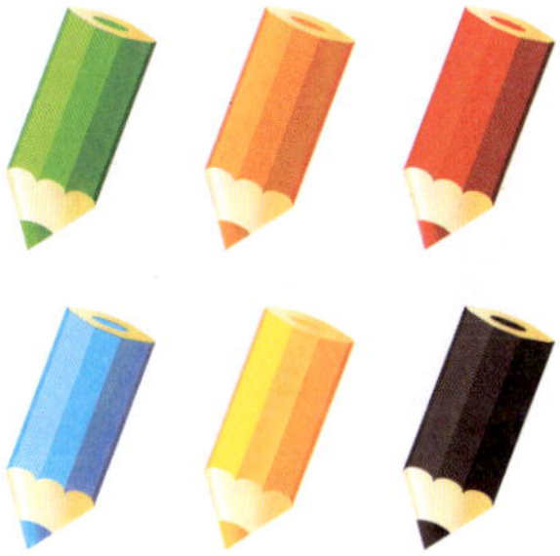

13

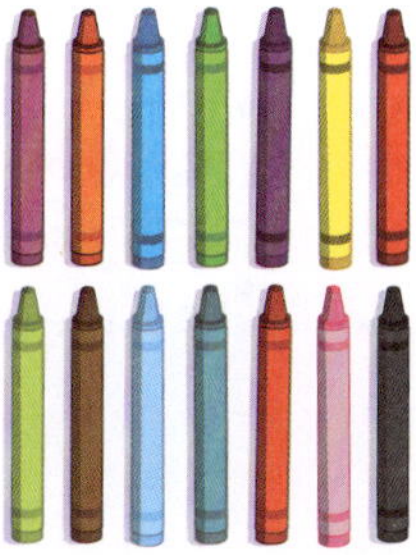

14

0 1 2 3 4 5 6 7 8 9 10

Practice tracing and writing the number.
Then count the buckets.

15 15

Fifteen

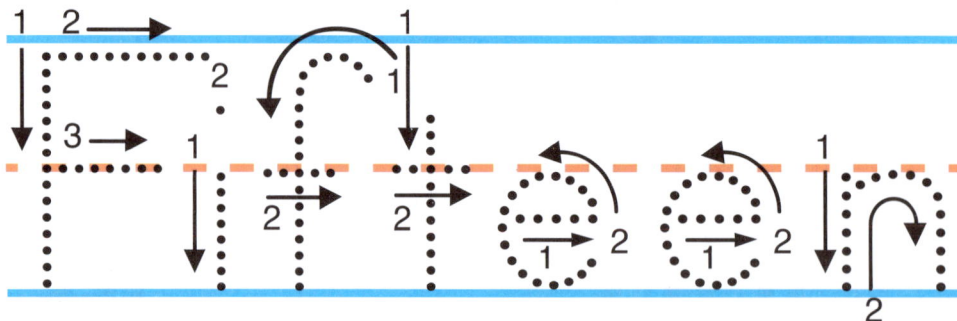

Counting backward, write the missing numbers on the blank lines.

15, ___ , 13

10, ___ , 8, 7

14, ___ , 12

___ , 11, 10

13, ___ , 11, ___ , 9

7, ___ , 5, 4

9, ___ , 7, ___ , 5

5, 4, ___ , 2

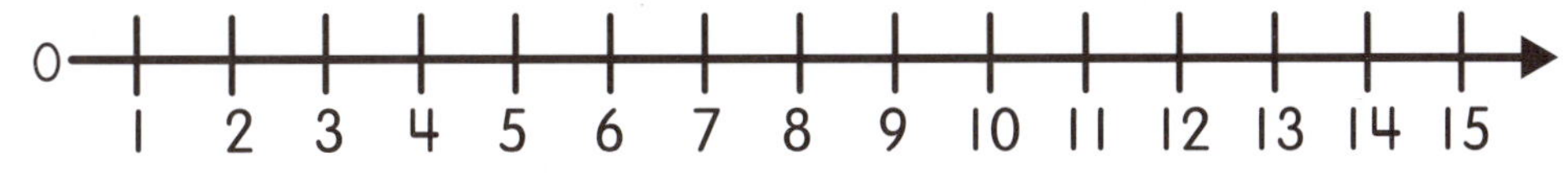

You did it!

0 1 2 3 4 5 6 7 8 9 10

Connect the dots in order 1-15 to finish the picture.

You did it!

Draw a circle around the **smallest** object in each column and a square around the **largest** .

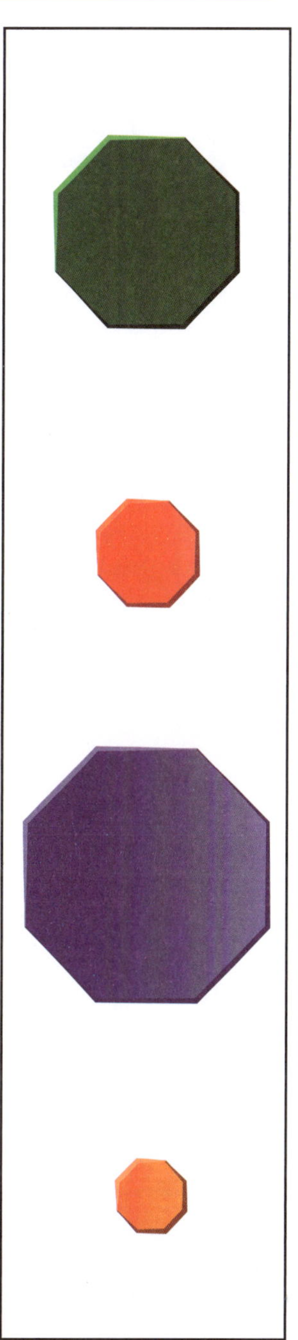

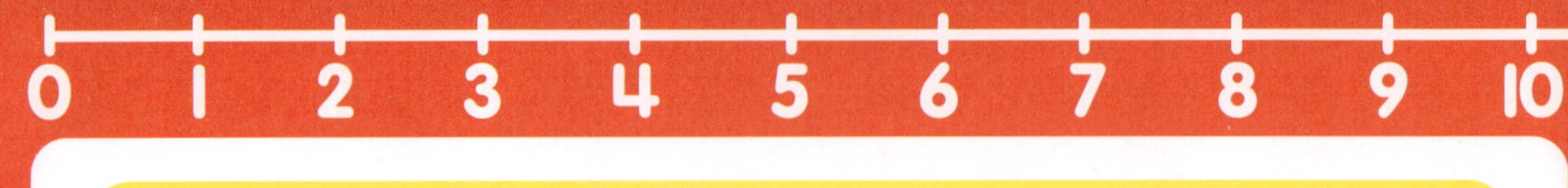

Practice tracing and writing the number.
Then count the baseballs.

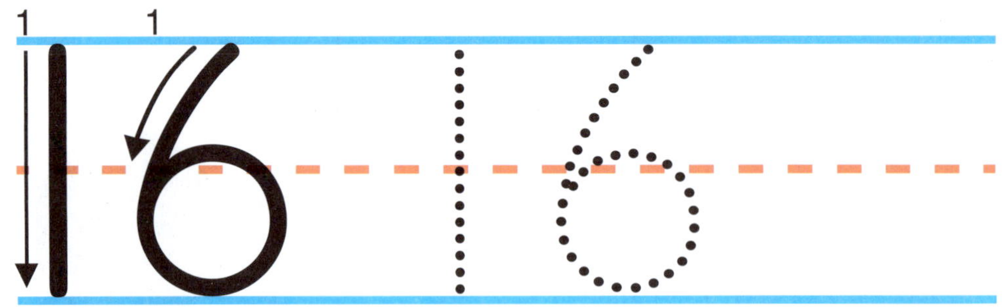

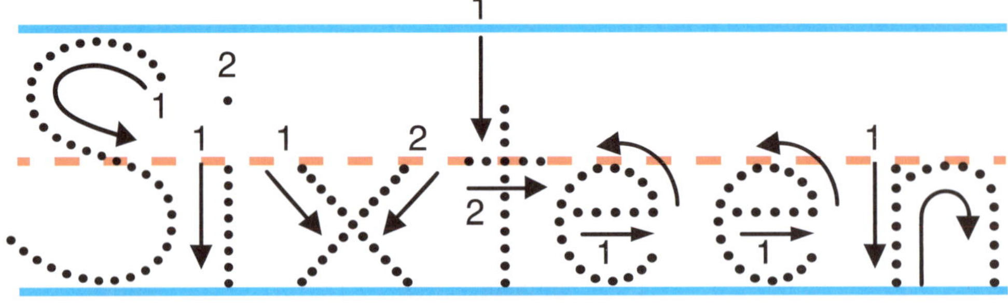

Color 16 candles and the number 16.

You did it!

Practice tracing and writing the number.
Then count the balloons.

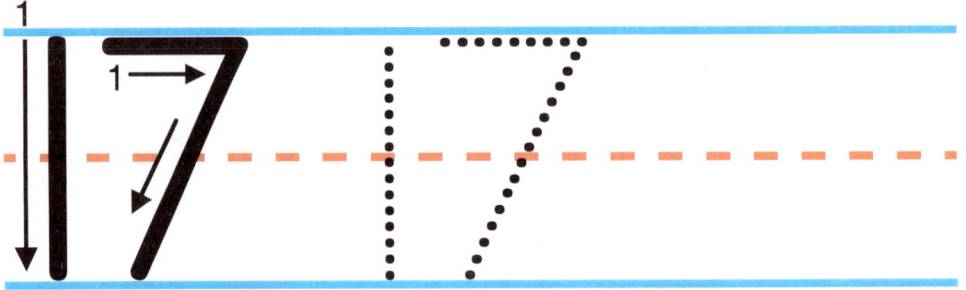

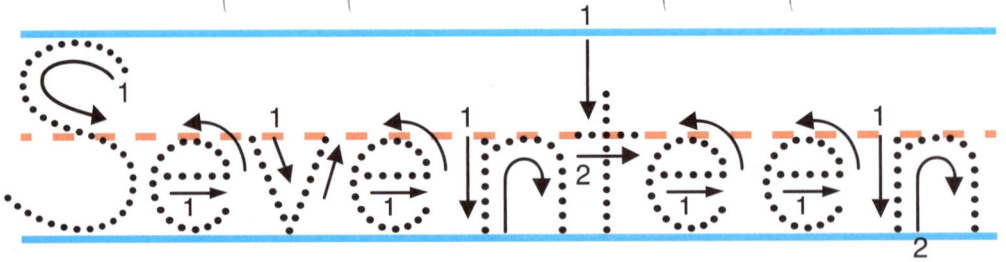

17 17

Seventeen

Put an X on the longest fence.
Circle the shortest fence.

0 1 2 3 4 5 6 7 8 9 10

Counting backward, write the missing numbers on the blank lines.

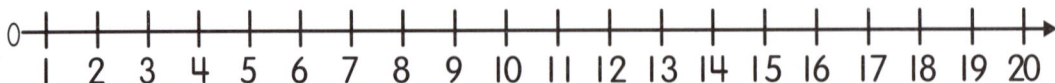

6, ___, 4, ___

16, ___, 14, ___

10, ___, ___, 7

11, 10, ___, 8

8, 7, ___, 5

20, ___, 18, ___

13, 12, ___, 10

18, ___, ___, 15

0 1 2 3 4 5 6 7 8 9 10 11 12 13 14 15 16 17 18 19 20

Practice tracing and writing the number.
Then count the pieces of pie.

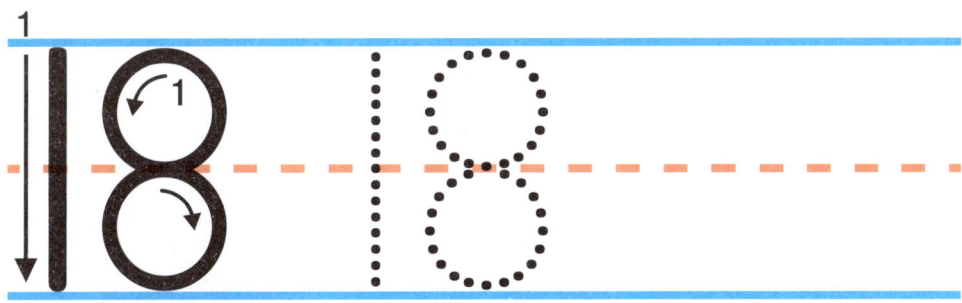

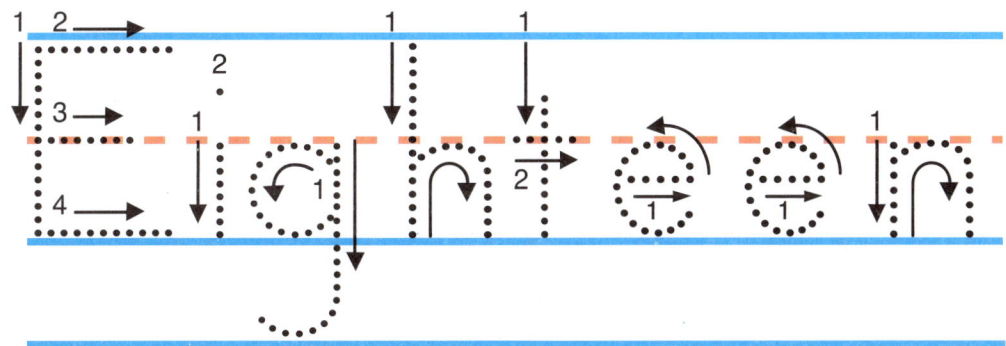

18 18

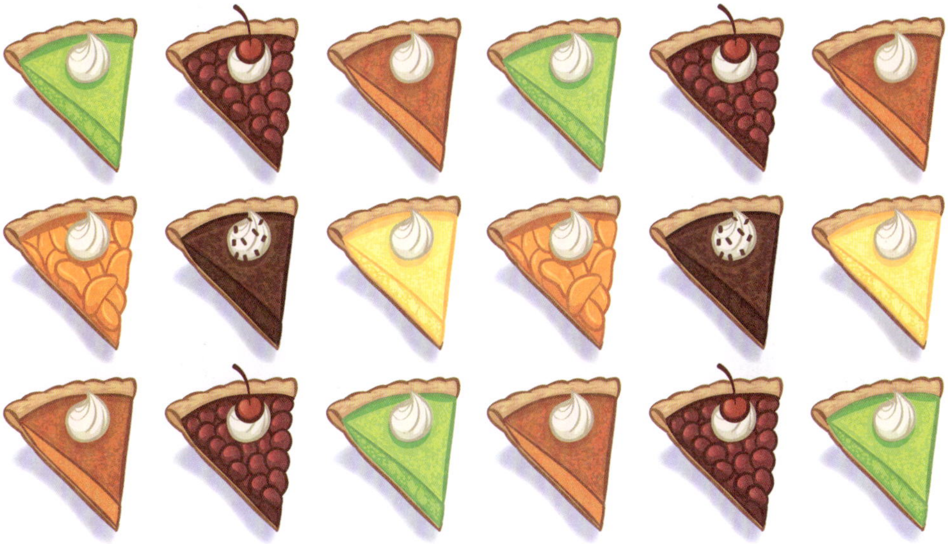

Eighteen

Put an X on the tallest tree in each row.
Circle the shortest tree in each row.

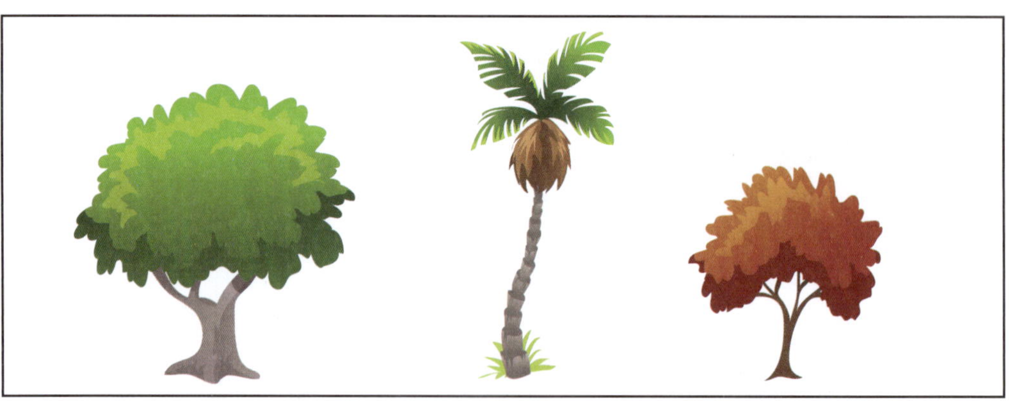

Practice tracing and writing the number.
Then count the whistles.

You did it!

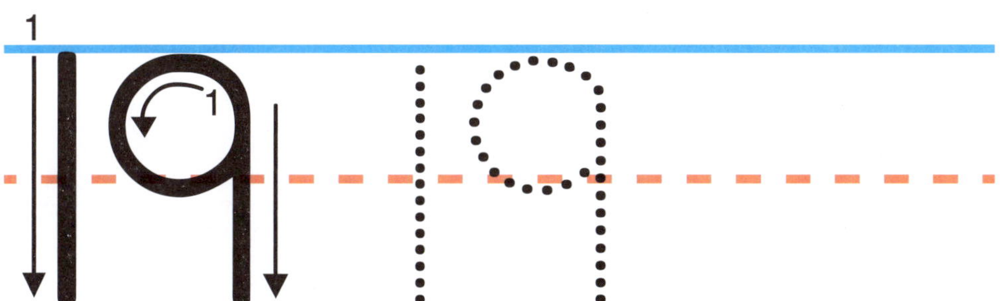

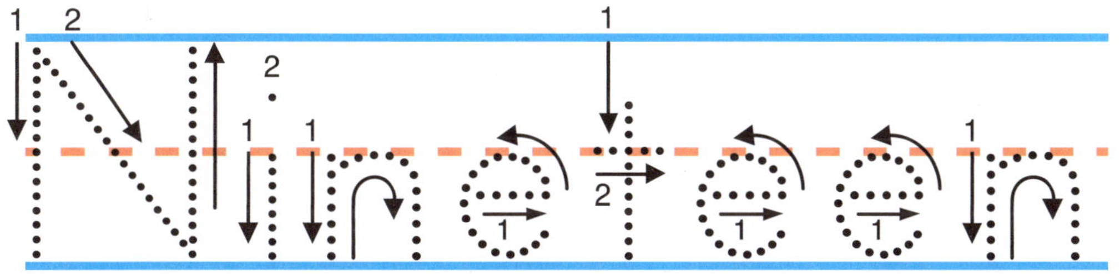

0 1 2 3 4 5 6 7 8 9 10

Counting forward, write the missing numbers on the blank lines.

17, ___ , 19

16, ___ , 18

14, ___ , 16

10, 11, ___

14, ___ , 16, ___

9, ___ , 11

6, ___ , 8, ___

11, ___ , 13, ___

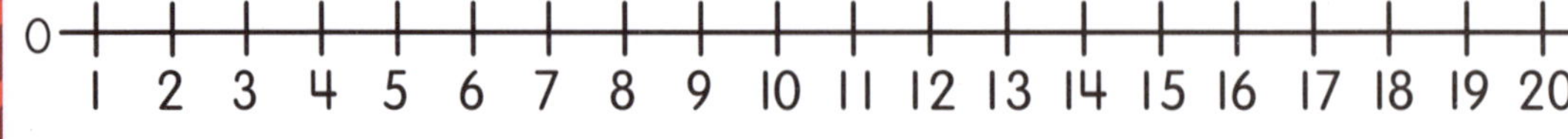

11 12 13 14 15 16 17 18 19 20

Practice tracing and writing the number.
Then count the dots.

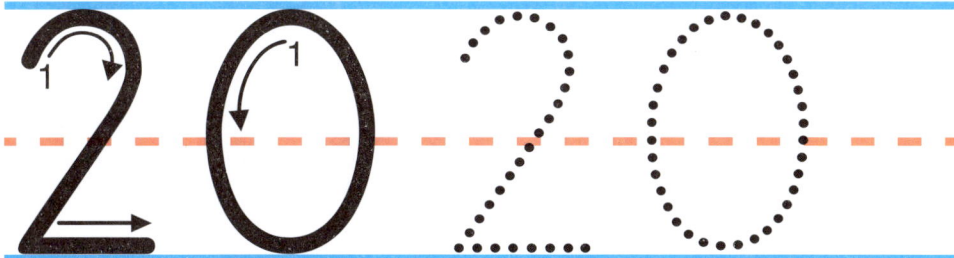

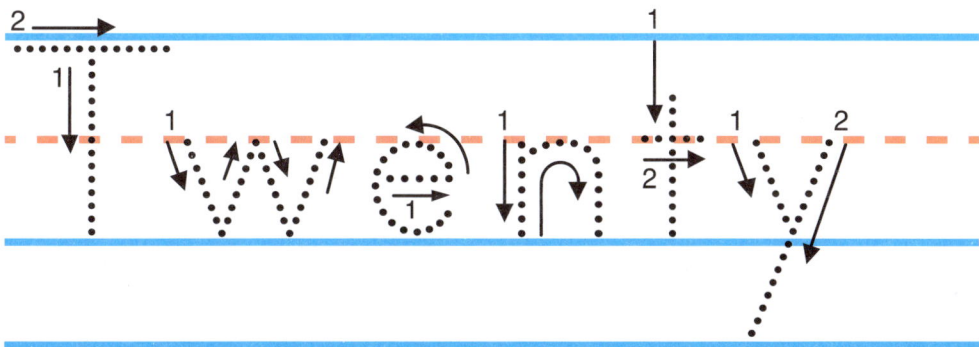

20 20

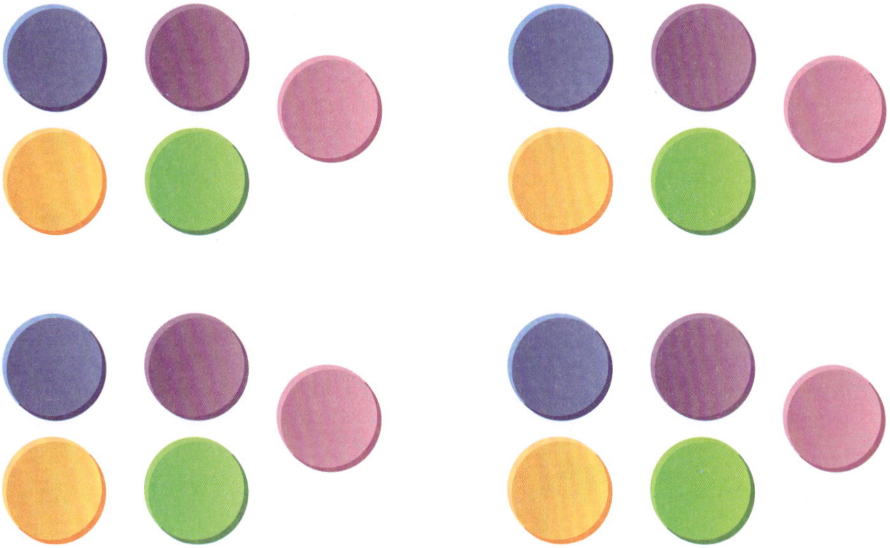

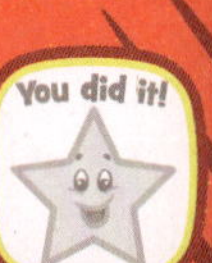

Twenty

0 1 2 3 4 5 6 7 8 9 10

Connect the dots in order 1-20 to finish the picture.

START
1
2
3
4
5
6
7
8
9
10
11
12
13
14
15
16
17
18
19
20